How to Get Your Ex Back

Elaborate Strategy How To Recognize Errors And Revitalize Yourself Within A Month. Surprise Your Former Partner And Successfully Rekindle The Relationship

(Make Him Beg To Be Your Boyfriend Again)

Hubert Zhang

TABLE OF CONTNET

Adjust A Few Things 1

Brief Messages To Her 6

Avoid Making These Errors 31

How To Modify Your Destructive Relationship Choice Patterns And Show True Love 57

Is Your Past Partner Willing To Give It Another Go? 82

What Caused The Split? 103

When Amicable Relationships Divorce 131

Adjust A Few Things

This is the most important step in getting your ex back since there is no other way to show them that you are serious about changing your life.

Remember that you're making these adjustments for yourself as much as for your ex-girlfriend, even though it can be difficult. You'll become more desirable to her and others when you develop personally.

Here are some guidelines for putting these changes into practice:

Identify the areas of your life that need development.

This could be anything, including your financial situation, appearance, or communication skills.

● Set smart, achievable goals. For example, instead of saying, "I want to be a better communicator," say, "I want to be able to listen to my ex-girlfriend without interrupting her, and I want to be able to express my feelings clearly and concisely."

● As a result, staying on course will be easier.

Take immediate action. Don't only think about changing things. Take immediate action.

Even little changes could accumulate over time to have a big effect.

Changes You Need to Make

● Improve Your Communication Skills: Learn to listen without talking in between, express your feelings clearly, and consider what your ex-girlfriend thinks.

● Let your emotions go wild. This means being open and honest with your ex-girlfriend about how you feel and willing to share those feelings. It also means offering sympathy and assistance.

● Concentrate on developing yourself. This could be going to therapy, reading self-help books, or taking classes.

You will be more attractive to your ex-girlfriend if you try to improve yourself.

● Become more physically beautiful. You do not need to become a supermodel as a result of this. However, it requires that you look your best and take after yourself.

Sort out your finances. To do this, you don't need to be affluent. It does, however, include having the resources necessary to settle your debts.

Making changes requires effort and time, but the benefits are valuable. As you develop personally, you'll draw in more attractive people, including your ex-girlfriend.

Extra Guidance

● Never be afraid to ask for help. See a friend, relative, coach, or therapist if you have trouble making changes independently. They can provide guidance and support.

● Never give up. Making adjustments requires work and patience. Don't give up if you don't get results straight away.

If you don't give up, you will eventually accomplish your goals.

Talk to Your Previous Girlfriend

After you've made some changes, it's important to reach out to your former partner in a considerate and courteous manner. You do not want to come across as pushy or desperate. Instead, you want to show her that you've changed and are a better person.

How to Get in Touch with Your Past Sweetheart

● Choose the right time and place. Don't contact her when she's upset or stressed out. Rather, choose a time when you are certain she will be receptive to your message.

● Swell and get syrupy. Stay away from sending her a long, convoluted text or email. Instead, be clear and concise.

● Be forthright and honest. Tell her your thoughts and the reason you're contacting her. Don't try to sidestep the problem or be smart.

● Respect her decision. Should she choose not to pursue a reunion and then honor her decision? Don't make any requests of her.

Brief Messages To Her

Here's an example of a brief but heartfelt message you could write to your ex:
"Hello [name of ex-girlfriend],

I realize it has been a while since our last conversation, but recently, you have been on my mind a lot.

I'm contacting you to see if you'd be interested in getting coffee sometime to catch up after I've changed my life and become a better person.

I understand if you're not interested, but please let me know if you are. There is no pressure in any case.

Best regards,

[Your name]"

If she says yes, you can arrange a coffee or another informal get-together. This is a fantastic chance to catch up and demonstrate to her your growth. Pay attention to her and convey your interest in what she has to say.

Respect her decision if she doesn't give you a positive response. Don't ask for anything from her. Keep in mind that you cannot make someone adore you.

Try again in a few days; she might change her mind. Women can be tough sometimes, but I promise this will work.

Making contact with your ex-girlfriend might be an intimidating and unsettling process. But it may be a constructive and constructive move forward if you're ready and know what to say.

VI. Develop Yourself as a Person

When people split up, it's usually because they truly want to be alone or make a statement before getting back together. Examine every situation in your life and figure out why your ex left if you want to have any chance of reconciling with him. Finding out why you two broke up can help you move on from the situation and provide you with some self-improvement ideas for when you want him back. Look for the bad seed that lost you, your ex, because, as is evident, no man has ever been known to up and leave his girlfriend while things are going well.

Self-improvement is meant to help you become more self-aware and realize that you are valuable and deserving of love, not to completely transform who you are.

Changing your lifestyle, going to the gym, and learning more about the other sex are all excellent methods to better yourself. You should engage in activities that enhance your sense of beauty and self-worth. This guideline ensures you can still complete yourself and be complimented by your better half, even though they are meant to do so.

VII. Do You Fit the No Contact Rule?

Don't waste time believing that your ex will miss you during this no-contact period, that it will be a lonely breakup, that he will second-guess his decision to end things with you, or even wonder how you are doing. These are the concerns of someone who doesn't know enough about the rule.

You shouldn't be bothered if his breakup with you has caused his life to become miserable; you are not responsible for it.

It's time to reconsider your reasons for wanting him back in your life if he begins acting pathetically toward you.

This guideline focuses entirely on how you can better your life without worrying about your former partner's location. He broke up with you for a sinister reason, which, more often than not, he will never immediately say. The most frequently used phrase in partnerships is "It's not you, it's me," which comes in second after "I love you." Don't let him turn you into a cliché so he can act as he pleases when he thinks he's made a mistake. You have an unlimited amount of time to choose your next move.

VIII. It's Not The Whole Plan for Reuniting With Your Ex-Boyfriend

The No Contact Rule is a highly specific component of the strategy of gaining back your ex; this does not mean that it is the only approach and that after you are done, the reunion is guaranteed. This step increases your chances of winning him back, but to win him back and keep him this time, you need to work on additional issues outside this article's scope.

You should utilize the No Contact period to figure out the whole plan for winning him back, but be careful not to lose too much time in your research and think about him all the time since you might find yourself tempted to talk to him. Get the facts, look over everything, and then determine if you want him back or gone permanently.

The No Contact Rule is a tool to help you work toward a broader goal of getting your ex back, but simply adhering to it won't guarantee that your relationship will return to normal.

There are numerous rules that the rule requires for it to work flawlessly, but they all come from one of the eight given in this chapter. Have a look at the regulations and keep them handy. If you do this, you will be well-positioned to begin and finish the time with success.

Chapter 5: Permitting Your Ex to Return to the Fold

Every couple is reminded of the wonderful times they had in the past by these events, so it is understandable why your ex would be open to getting back to you. However, as they say, "You Must Go Slow." Furthermore, you at least feel that you are with each other because you love and understand each other. Joining the team makes space for a get-together and conversation.

The first thing you should know is that once you meet, you should never begin placing blame. Recall the best times you two can still share. Arrange for outings and walks in the outdoors as you mend your shared injuries. Make sure, particularly during this trying period, that you are not the victim of careless errors that you know annoy your partner.

Seeing Your Former Partner for the First Time After the Break

Your ex may desire you back if they try to meet with you. Your ex is attempting to examine unresolved feelings, at the very least. Above all, take your time and let things unfold naturally.

Try to propose a quick and sweet place for your ex to meet. Lunch or coffee will allow the reunion date to go swiftly and end before things get awkward, so both options are good. You want to introduce yourself to your ex in tiny doses at first. You'll always leave your ex wanting more of you if you don't give away too much and terminate the date fairly swiftly.

Additional Brilliant Strategies for Reuniting with Your Former Partner or Girlfriend

Reversing your breakup ultimately comes down to mindset. Additionally, it's about focusing on strategies to make your ex desire you again. There is a time and place for retreat strategies, fast reconnection tactics, and no-contact policies on the path to reconciliation. Ensure you understand what each of these terms means and what stage of the breakup you may be in. This makes it the ideal permission for your ex to return without any hassles.

If you know somewhere they're talking about when they start talking about travel, that's the ideal moment to introduce yourself. You talk about your experiences, your travels, and the lessons you discovered. As a result, you become someone they can relate to, and you've just established your first point of contact.

But what if you don't agree with what they are talking about? Be at ease, my friend. We're not trying to make things seem alike. This isn't a competition. You can change the topic of discussion to something you are interested in if you can't relate to the one being discussed. Perhaps you ask, "That sounds great. Have any of you ever been to...?" and then change the subject to something more familiar.

Being the most popular person at the party is not the goal of this whole thing. It's to create sincere relationships with other individuals. And to accomplish that, you must be true to who you are. "We must be authentic to be accepted by others. Not the idea of ourselves that we think we should be, but who we are," writes Brené Brown in her book "The Gifts of Imperfection" (2010).

As a result, you mingle and form bonds during the celebration. Gaining more connections through shared laughs, stories, and experiences brings you one step closer to your objective of growing your network. You leave the evening with new friendships made, as well as a feeling of fulfillment and achievement.

What if, together, we decided to start growing our networks? How about we transform this recuperation process into exploring self-improvement and learning? We will keep doing this until that comfort zone is a continent full of fascinating people and experiences rather than just an island.

Opening yourself up to meeting new people is a bridge of possibilities that will lead you to exciting destinations, as Keith Ferrazzi emphasized in his book "Never Eat Alone" (2005). "In an era when networking has become a vital currency, having a rich network of diverse connections can be a powerful engine of opportunity." Every new person you meet is a fresh book full of tales to delve into, a fresh map of paths to take, and you never know—you might even find the link that brings you and your ex back together.

But keep in mind that the purpose of this period is to broaden your horizons and enhance your life with new experiences and relationships rather than to frantically run to your ex. You change during this process, becoming more intriguing, self-assured, and enriched. Who could resist that, after all?

This chapter has shown you how widening improves your quality of life, in addition to being a tactic to get your ex back. We've discussed how to approach unfamiliar situations, discuss, and form relationships. You get closer to being the best version of yourself with each step and action you take.

But we must not stop here. As we proceed, every chapter takes us one step closer to the objective of a full recovery. What do you think about proceeding to the next phase?

The next chapter will delve into the intriguing concept of the 'magic of absence.' Is less truly more? Is it true that being apart can intensify love? How can we make use of this on the path to recovery?

Sometimes, we must go back one step to go ahead two on the road to recovery. Silence truly does sometimes speak louder than words. However, how? When? Why? We'll find all those answers in our next chapter, my friend. And I can't wait for us to continue on this path of development and exploration together.

Are you prepared to go on in this adventure and solve the riddle of the "magic of absence" to learn how we can take advantage of it? I hope to see you in the upcoming chapter if the response is affirmative. As always, I'm here for you, and together, we'll find the right path to a full recovery and significant personal development.

Section Two

Step-by-Step Strategies for the No Contact Rule

Now that we better understand our motivations, let's discuss our plans in more detail. Selecting a time frame is the first action that needs to be taken and the first step in your plan.

#1: SET A TIME FRAME AND REMEMBER IT

This is probably going to be the simplest portion of the entire process! Consider this your starting point, your preparation for the most significant endeavor of your life. The tasks you accomplish during this period will be very useful for you in the future. Thus, my dear, this is crucial stuff. As a general rule of thumb, three alternatives exist for how long you want to spend in the No Contact phase of your relationship.

The following three are typically the most beneficial:

21 days

thirty days

forty-five days

The duration you select will be determined by how the relationship ended. Depending on how injured you are, yes. You will have to wait longer to contact him, the worse it will be. It's more about forming new habits than how much time you spend on each plan component. It's probably common knowledge by now that any kind of new habit needs at least 21 days to form. Whatever the reason, if we want to go jogging every day, it will take our minds at least 21 consecutive days to process the idea that we're doing something different and that we mean business. It just seems to operate this way; I'm not sure why. So there's no point in battling it!

You won't experience any more or less difficulty in the future if;

- You're a creature of habit and take great pleasure in the framework that new routines provide for you.
- You are probably the type of person who looks around the bookshop for reference books, makes thoughtful notes to oneself, and then follows through on them.
- You're the type of person who enjoys trying new things. Take the gluten-free trend, for instance, and stick with it.

Simply select a time range and record your start and finish dates in a designated spot. It's a terrific idea and sometimes fun to design a little picture and save it as the backdrop and wallpaper on your phone. Assuming, for example, that your expiration date is October 12th, you might put this date on a piece of paper and either circle it with an amusing image or simply underline it all in cheerful, vibrant colors. After that, you can check it to easily track how long you have left.

For at least two-thirds of the process, if you do not work well under routine, this will be a battle you simply have to push through! I swear, everything will be fine.

2 Not a phone call

It should go without saying, as you have probably surmised, and I am not kidding when I say this is on the list. For whatever reason, don't give him a call. If you own one of his CDs, that doesn't bother me. It doesn't bother me if he left his best running shoes at your place. If you don't think they'll be stolen or rained on, you may just put them out on the covered porch if it's that much of a worry and it's his most valuable item. You're just keeping silent for now; you're not attempting to hurt him in any way.

You hear me? Not a single call at all? None. This will sometimes be challenging, particularly in this social media age when asking someone what they're doing with a short text or brief Facebook message is so simple. Well, a phone call is so much more personal. It conveys your longing for him and a depth of loneliness that is endearing but will probably come out as desperate. That is not what we desire! You don't need him to watch that Netflix movie with you, sweetness; we want him to think of us as self-sufficient and not reliant. You watch that with a girlfriend or alone, excluding him for now. Any indications of your call that appear on his phone indicate that he is finding it difficult to adjust to your newfound free time, which will turn him off rather than make him miss you. You two needed a break since, for whatever reason, you two broke up. Whether or not he wants it, let's give it to him.

Now, this is a different story—oh wait, no, it's not—if you notice that he has phoned YOU! No phoning him back, please. It makes no difference if he leaves you a voicemail; feel free to listen if so. But don't give him a callback. You won't call him back if his car broke down outside your house or his puppy is in the hospital. Here, we have a plan, and we're going to stick with it. Check your finish date when you feel like you're having trouble. Already, you've come that much closer. You can get in touch again after that date, but if you abandon the phone calls before then, nothing will function. Love, keep up your strength!

#3: Modify His Phone Number

For many women, taking this step is crucial; for others, it should go without saying! Change his name to something else by going into the phone's settings. Many women find it most appealing to have him adopt the moniker "NO MA'AM." It's straightforward, endearing, and persistent. This is a gentle reminder to stick with your No Contact time; you are not required to answer that call or text.

#4: Don't text.

You will most likely find it most difficult to break this behavior. You should text him if you know he's there when your car breaks down, or you happen to pass past your favorite restaurant. Since you already purchased his fundraising ticket, you should remind him that your little sister has a Friday night recital and inquire whether he still wants to accompany you. Just don't do it, as tempting as it may be. Consider this a positive indication that things are going well if he recalls that you had a prearranged date and feels like texting or phoning to check if you still want him to go. Don't text him back, though.

Avoid Making These Errors

If you want to have a chance of winning your ex back, there are some things you should avoid doing. Making these errors could force your ex to give up on you completely.

Keep your cool both during and after the breakup.

Don't yell, lose your temper, or go crazy. Keep your feelings contained. You will not succeed if you cry or lose your cool with him. That will only make him flee from you even more.

When you behave coolly, the odds seem to be more equal. Make an effort to act differently from what he probably expects from you. You will arouse his curiosity. He's probably wondering why you don't appear to be as angry or devastated as he had anticipated. If you want to win him back later on, this will pique his interest, which is a more promising response than sympathy or dislike.

With all the poise, maturity, and composure you possess, accept the breakup. He will remember you with gratitude and respect if you behave with grace and dignity despite the hurt.

Don't show that you're unhappy.

You likely believe communicating with your former partner is essential to let him know you're still available. You believe you need to make it simple for him to contact you again. Relationship experts, however, advise being careful not to come out as miserable.

This will just make your ex feel further distant from you if he perceives you as needy or desperate. Needy girls are viewed as ugly by most men. Don't text or call him like you have nothing better to do with your time. Do not tell him this, even if it were true.

Don't implore or grovel for him to reconsider the relationship.

Don't ask him to stay with you. Your dignity and sense of self-respect will be lost.

Don't act as though you couldn't survive without him. He's not going to take you back with you like this. All he'll see in you is insecurity, weakness, and lack of beauty.

You do not want to play the pity game with your guy. Is it something you want back in your relationship if he changes his mind out of sympathy? A relationship is better and stronger when its foundation is built on love, trust, respect, appreciation, understanding, and a desire for companionship. You don't want your connection to be based mostly on sympathy.

If your ex decides not to end things with you out of sympathy, you might have to deal with severe consequences. He'll probably regret this choice later on. He'll realize that his acceptance of you again was motivated entirely by the wrong things. He might even blame you. He'll probably want to leave again.

You are essentially keeping your ex-hostage if you yell, weep, or threaten to harm yourself if he doesn't want to get back together. You're employing emotional blackmail and manipulation. He will probably grow bitter and angry if he does agree to make amends with you. He will likely end things with you once more.

Refrain from letting him tramp all over you.

Don't give up everything in an attempt to patch things up.

You could believe that you can win him back by complying with your boyfriend's requests. It's going to be a rough ride. Never give up on your needs, ambitions, ideals, or desires to reconcile with your former partner. If you allow yourself to become a doormat for him, he is likely to lose all his respect for you. You will probably come to despise yourself. Respect-deficient relationships are unlikely to succeed.

For a relationship to succeed, you must be able and willing to resolve your differences. Both parties ought to be prepared to give in. A partnership is imbalanced if only one person is willing to make compromises. It will eventually go.

Put a temporary stop on all correspondence with your former partner.

This period off is known as the "no contact rule" by relationship specialists. As per the guidelines, you need to stop communicating with your ex in any way. This covers every kind of communication. Don't give me a call. Avoid texting. Never send private messages via Facebook. Avoid contacting him on Twitter or any other similar social media sites. Don't even go out with friends in common in the hopes of running into him.

After the breakup, you and your ex will be quite emotional. It will be challenging for you to make well-considered or logical conclusions. Cut off all correspondence with one another. This is going to help you de-stress. This will enable you to rationally assess your respective positions.

You will also have more time to heal if you follow the no-touch rule. Breakups are challenging. You treat each other badly and cause each other pain. It takes time for tempers to cool down. You need time to think things over. It takes time for you to recover. You'll encounter the same problems if you try to make amends without pausing to reflect on your life's lessons. You will encounter the same contentious issues once more.

You must give time to go by. You'll be able to see the split more objectively and constructively after taking some time apart. You can only expect to be able to communicate with one another without experiencing intense emotions if you give each other some breathing room.

You won't be able to make the effort to make things right until then.

Reevaluating your life will also be aided by the no-contact policy. It provides context for the situation. It allows you to positively alter how you live your life. This is a crucial matter. The time away should have made you a happier and more beautiful woman, should you ultimately decide you want your ex back. Don't rush anything. For fun, form amicable relationships.

You never know; he might want to see you again if you can pique his attention. Alternatively, you can request to see him when the moment is appropriate.

View your former partner.

Take care that you don't call the event a date. You don't want to give him a defensive feeling. You don't want him to know you're trying to get him back. You want him to think of you as a buddy prepared to accept responsibility for previous transgressions and apologize when necessary.

Make subtle use of the time to increase interest. This shouldn't be too challenging. In the past, you were both drawn to one another. Rekindling the attraction shouldn't be hard, especially because you've changed so much that he will undoubtedly find you appealing.

Don't be serious; be lighthearted. You can offer a heartfelt apology if you caused someone great pain. Next, proceed. Don't let the conversation center on the breakup. Think of your previous relationship with him as ended. Remain charming, kind, and gracious. Find subtle methods to present yourself to him as the lovely woman he once fell in love with. Put on an outfit that he adored or wear perfume. Tell him about the good times you had together.

If you both find this first "non-date" enjoyable enough, you might wish to go out together again. Maintain an amicable atmosphere. Dinner, a concert, or a movie are all options. Maintaining equilibrium and trying to reacquaint oneself with one another and rebuild your friendship is crucial.

Remember that this is a new beginning. You are embarking on a brand-new, sober chapter in your life, not attempting to patch up your past relationship.

Before you try, you never know what you're capable of.

It surely sounds like torture to be informed that you have to avoid speaking with your ex for 30 days. I'm sure you believe you are incapable of doing it. Your ex is someone you want and need in your life. How are you going to get by without speaking with them? How are you going to get through the day without hearing from them? Isn't the real result going to be to push them further away? See how this all turns out differently than you anticipated by watching.

I know you feel like you can't do this and are hurt from missing them. They won't require your assistance if you relinquish all touch and control. Do you recognize this? The reality is that you don't know what you're capable of until you try. This holds for all aspects of life but becomes especially true while trying to get your ex back. You're going to be a much happier person due to their perception of you being completely different.

You Can Achieve Your Goals by Doing This

The No Contact Rule is a tool to help you get your ex back, not a means of punishment. It defies the customary conduct each of us has employed when compulsively hatching plans to win our ex back. That wasn't a very successful outcome, was it? You discover that you are far more capable of change than you ever imagined when you allow yourself to gather your thoughts and begin afresh. By applying the No Contact Rule, you will reconnect with your true self and win your ex back.

You CAN do this, even if it's hard at first. Take it as it comes; thirty days isn't that long! Take each day as it comes, and use the time to improve yourself. Put them out of your mind and out of sight, and remember that their purpose is to support you in making the necessary changes in your life.

You will get your ex back, but it won't require ongoing effort. You will discover the wonderful bonus of being happier as a result of keeping your focus on the goal and remembering why you are doing all of this!

It hurts even to think your ex is with someone else. However, reality is not as bad as we make it out to be. We'll discuss it later, but for now, let's examine how it feels in your stomach when you find out that your ex is dating someone else;

If I don't do something right away, they'll fall in love with this new person and never think about me again.

I'll do everything for them, including begging, playing pathetic, telling them how much I care, and caving into all of their requests (being a doormat). If they don't open the door, I'll stand outside all day and give them calls and texts.

I have to tell my ex-boyfriend how completely improper this new person is for them and what a huge mistake it is for them to be dating this... (INSERT DEROGATORY REMARK).

If you haven't already noticed, your mind and instincts worry when you find your ex dating someone new. When you're stressed, you usually do all the things mentioned above.

Your ex is most likely having an affair on the rebound.

Furthermore, the majority of rebound relationships end abruptly. Rebound relationships, albeit painful, are a common way for people to deal with breakups. It's one of the least effective methods to move on for your benefit. Therefore, don't assume that they'll move on from you just because they're in a rebound relationship.

It just says the contrary. It suggests that while in this rebound relationship, they find it difficult to let go of their hurt and move on. They will, therefore, take longer to get over you.

The most important thing to accomplish is to let go of your ex's rebound relationship.

Under no circumstances should you advise your ex to break up with their rebound partners. Let them come up with it.

They are trying to fill the huge gap in their lives that they experienced after breaking up with someone new.

They will usually break up as soon as they understand a rebound relationship won't meet their needs.

Deadly Error #6: Calling names and getting angry

People who used to call their former names during arguments often do so to express their rage or dissatisfaction. Additionally, it's normal if you both make constant threats to break up.

Calling your ex derogatory names will only make her less interested in you. But it's difficult to determine whether your body is in fight or flight mode and whether you're still in a panic.

If you verbally attacked one another or lost your cool during an argument or fight, there's a good chance that your instinct will tell you to behave that way after the relationship ends.

Perhaps your first thought is that this is just another argument or confrontation. And when you tell your ex you're angry, they'll calm down and say they want to make up.

Much like the last time, you two battled.

It hardly ever works like this. Only if your ex is sincere about the breakup will getting upset make them think that calling it quits on your relationship was the right move.

If you get offended, they'll be reminded of all the ugly fights and arguments that eroded the foundation of your relationship.

You'll remind them that you two don't understand each other, and they'll think you're not the right person for them.

If this resonates with you, this is a great opportunity to recognize and address any unhealthy habits you may have developed.

Arguments shouldn't always end in shouting, violence, or derogatory remarks. I believe that making an effort to acquire useful communication skills would be beneficial. Go through communication-related books, and if needed, get help. If you're having trouble deciding what to do next and feeling lost or confused, you might want to consider getting relationship coaching.

Deadly Error #7: Fixation and Misunderstanding

The infatuation that follows a horrible breakup is probably the toughest part.

Your mind is always racing, trying to figure out the best way to win your ex back as soon as possible.

Your mind is aching for a failsafe plan. It seeks guarantees that your connection with your former spouse will stay harmonious.

It will ask questions like these:

Will my former spouse come back?

"Does my ex still miss me?"

Is he still the one who loves me?

How can I get him back to me faster?

Will she start dating someone already?

Now that she's gone on a date, is it over?

"Does this suggest he is over me? He looked cheerful in a picture he shared on Instagram."

"On Snapchat, my ex added me. Does he intend to return if he says this? Is it okay if I reach out to him?

If you jot down every question that comes to mind, you'll discover they are virtually useless.

I say this because it is impossible to know the right answers to these questions—questions that neither you nor anybody else can know the answers to.

They're all worried about what your ex is thinking. Nobody can tell you what your ex is thinking or what will happen in the future unless they are the oracle.

These queries are your mind trying to accomplish an impossibility; your instinct has set your thinking on a mission.

Imagine that your instincts tell your mind to do the following. Imagine that your mind is a machine that will try to solve whatever difficulties you present it with.

"Find a way to guarantee I'll get my ex back." Please, please, please save my ex from going away. Please resolve this as soon as possible, because my ex might find someone else. If you don't, it will be hard for me to survive (and, by extension, YOU).

Can you see where this is going wrong?

You are motivated to come up with a way to take away someone's free will because of your intuition and anxiety. Furthermore, it lacks the requisite length of time. Additionally, the threat to your survival comes from your impulses. That makes sense as to why your thoughts are racing.

These questions won't get your ex to leave on their own. But when your mind is working overtime, it is more likely to make mistakes.

Most of the mistakes above are the product of ill-considered, hurried decisions. A paper that emerged in a publication illustrates how worry can impair judgment.

How To Modify Your Destructive Relationship Choice Patterns And Show True Love

Regardless of our awareness of it or not, we have all had or will continue to have dysfunctional relationships that we keep repeating. When they initially come to see me, many of my clients are unaware of their "destructive choice patterns" and are shocked to learn that they have done the same things to achieve the same results.

Exercise

Try to keep in mind the "ix" scenarios that arose from your previous relationships that led to conflicts, and write down what you now desire.

Make sure you avoid using negative statements. For instance, if your ex cheated on you, write "I want a partner who is a matchmaker" instead of "I don't want someone who cheats."

Be as specific as possible. If you want someone to be gentle, don't just put them there; also, express what gentleness means.

Focus on yourself if you are already in a relationship rather than worrying about what the other person should or shouldn't do.

It means looking hard at your life in the present, the things that make you feel good about yourself, and the things that make you uncomfortable or unhappy. You have to face the "truth" about your past that you carry with you when you are not focused on someone else.

For each of the five states, complete the following: begin with the first state you've written, then proceed to 1, 2, and 3 before moving on to the next.

Read each state aloud until you can hear your voice.

Then ask yourself, where is this coming from? Is it coming from a distant past (your parents' relationship, what you went through as a child, what your classmates projected onto you by how they treated you, etc.) or a recent past (breakup, divorce, etc.)?

Permit yourself to feel the pain and the emotions. You must bravely face the pain and the emotions, realizing that they are less powerful than your true self.

Positive and negative feelings can be the guiding light to our true selves. If you find yourself crying, don't feel ashamed or embarrassed.

Teachers could very well be the therapy you require. Often, acknowledging that you feel a certain way enables you to go naturally from being stuck in that condition to a more serene and pure state.

Many self-help books, workbooks, and professional publications might assist you in dealing with certain difficult pain situations. Avoid books that only discuss a specific pain issue without guiding you on how to treat it.

Avoid becoming an "expert" on your particular "problem"; instead, move past it (which is why it's called a "past") and consult a physician.

Suppose you decide too are already seeing a counselor or therapist you should be able to see a change in your life within the third/fourth visit (you are much happier, more relaxed and feel that you are truly leaving your past behind and stepping into the present). If after five sessions you don't see a change, even a slight one, then change your counselor or therapist.

Ask yourself what steps you are taking to recreate your past.

It may be difficult for most people to realize that we do things on an unconscious level and are not even conscious of what we do. Still, when you start to be aware of what you are doing to create your experiences, you are also beginning to be aware of what you can do to change future outcomes.

If you are in a relationship, there is a reason why you and your partner continue to have the same arguments, conflicts, and stories. There is also a reason why you keep attracting the same kind of men (different faces, but same stories).

Theother person mayhavehisorher own "issues" but youdidnotjuststumbleinto this personandrelationship, yourunconsciousradarcarefully searched for a partnerwithspecificcharacteristics. Recognizethe "issues" andmake a consciousdecisiontochangehow you react.Thisappliestoallyourrelationships (family, friends, co-workersetc).

Finally, ask yourself: "What have I done to prepare myself for someone who is...? I mean, a monogram, a financially responsible person, an organized, health-conscious person, entertaining and engaging, sexually fulfilling, potentially a health-conscious person, etc., if that's what you have written down."

In a relationship, ask yourself, "What am I doing, or not doing, that I am accusing him or her of not doing for me?

If you have trouble controlling your emotions, find it difficult to be happy, or have very low self-esteem, you should work on it to attract someone's attention.

Get some advice and reconstruct your savings and investing program if you are excessively impulsive, too laid back, or too irresponsible regarding finances. If you are too reserved and "boring," develop your playful side to attract someone who will bring more excitement into your life.

If you wish to meet someone with healthy habits, visit your home or apartment, tidy the closets, stock up on healthier foods, and establish a fitness regimen you can stick to.

If you have a fantasy life but your real life is all in your head, put in the effort to locate and join a group of like-minded seekers.

Your spiritual life thrives most when it is in the company of others. Enhance your bedrock skills if you desire more intimacy in your relationships than in the past. You can do this by finding a book, attending a tantra sex education class, working individually with an intimacy counselor, or engaging in other therapeutic activities.

The most important thing to remember is that you will undoubtedly become a better version of yourself if you commit to improving yourself. Furthermore, a better you will draw in a better partner and develop a better relationship.

If you discover someone dedicated to his or her personal growth, you will have already overcome many of the difficulties that many couples encounter. Not only will your relationship improve, but your partner will also feel pressured to reach your emotional and spiritual maturity level.

A word of caution: if your partner grows and becomes more confident and you don't, you will both feel uncomfortable in the relationship and may even become controlling towards others closer to you. This applies to both close friends and traditional relationships.

Regardless of how you react to someone or something that someone says or does, ask yourself why you feel the way you do.

Because you have made a conscious decision or invested effort to focus on yourself, your feelings will lead to the source of your "discomfort." Next, decide consciously to alter the outcome by altering your response.

Act immediately. Whatever you believe you are capable of, start. Your dreams are your soul's beautiful, powerful, and magical desires. Sobegin your dreamrelationshipnow...

The sexual frontiers are opening!

Thus, you and Mr. Wonderful are currently in a situation where the chemistry is exploding, and you cannot keep your hands off each other.

You've been out at least a few times, and the responsibility you bear seems to be igniting a "green light." Before you rush to the bedroom (or any other provocative sexual location!), ask yourself these questions to avoid getting hurt and to ensure that this is the right time for you to get naked:

Why are we desiring sex right now? What motivates us?

1. Do I feel emotionally and physically safe with him? Can I trust him enough to give my body and emotions to him?

2. Do I feel taken care of by him? Is there more innate curiosity and tenderness in

me in areas other than sex? Does he respond negatively to me?

3. Can I be myself around him freely? Are I feeling good about myself when I'm with him? Do I like the man based on what I've learned about him thus far?

4-Are we able to speak honestly with one another? Have we all engaged in sufficient self-disclosure to feel comfortable with one other? Have we been able to show each other affection this much yet?

5. Is there demonstrated loyalty and dependability? Do I have a personality? Do we have mutual respect and support?

Additional Tips Before Dipping In

1. Verify that you have discussed your sexual histories and have engaged in

discussions regarding sexually transmitted diseases, safe sex, and beliefs regarding monogamy versus non-monogamy. It doesn't necessarily need to do that, even if it seems to take away some of the excitement.

Participate in the "erotĖcforreplay" conversation by sharing your sexual values, preferences, attitudes, and dreams to deepen intimacy and learn more about each other. PARTITION FROM THE "turn-on" AND "build-up."

2. It could be beneficial to communicate with prospective employers about something like "I'm very interested in you, but I don't have sex until I know someone." Such a blunt, up-front, and assertive statement will likely turn off

those who could match your ideal client. Those who don't.

Many men who "abandon marriage" may come your way, but they weren't meant to be, and it now takes a lot of time and energy for you to pursue your issues. Remember, it's quality, not quantity.

3. While you're in the "waiting phase" and shielding yourself from sexual encounters, persistently create a "tease" and try to make your partner aware that you're still interested in him and find him engaging in a respectful flirtation.

Many gay men have been forced to say they are "no sex" and may be sensitive to "sexual harassment," so they play a lot of "poisoned games" to keep the friendship alive.

4-Although it was suggested that having sex right away could aid in determining whether you are sexually compatible, remember that everything depends on your individual needs and what you believe to be most significant.

Additionally, keep in mind that sex tends to be more romantic and fulfilling when a foundation of emotional intimacy has already been established and that it gets hotter the longer a couple is together (practice makes perfect!).

Ultimately, regardless of how much effort you put up to be a successful dater, there will inevitably be instances where you make a mistake, exhibit poor judgment, or the other person leaves without explanation. Remember to be kind to yourself and that you are human.

Acknowledge the mistakes you made and rectify your data plan. You don't have any control over how the other guy acts.

Remember that many people find that sex is a loaded issue, and unresolved sexuality issues can be a major source of guilt for people who believe that they have good dating prospects and who break off their relationships soon after they begin.

Keep your heart safe, remain patient, and never give up hope that your Mr. Right is still out there—the time hasn't come yet.

Keep This in Mind

You have a positive outlook on the breakup. You've been by yourself for some time, learning about yourself and improving. You now want to introduce this new you to your ex, who knows nothing but your old self. How are you doing now?

1. Understanding that loving someone is a choice

How many times have they considered ending things? Instead of leaving, they decided to look for reasons to stay. There won't be many times when you're considering leaving because you've decided to love someone the more you put into developing and maintaining a relationship.

2. Being able to forgive is not a sign of weakness.

As I previously said, you should be prepared to forgive and move on if you choose to go back. What do you think? It is not a weakness to forgive. Everyone makes errors, but only the courageous choose to move past their mistakes and face the future.

Not just you have transformed.

Don't return with the mindset that you are the only one who has cleaned up. Proceed there with composure. This is because you must also develop the ability to accept those changes.

Most people enjoy returning to past relationships, but it is not the best approach. It's as simple as adopting the proper mindset, and things will fall into place. Not miraculously, but as a gradual process.

It's Time To Make Friends Now

You buddy your way to your ex instead of hopping, stepping, and jumping back to them. I mean being a true friend and doing everything related to friendship, not just being friendly. To find a way into your ex's heart, tell your hormones to calm down and apply the following stops.

Show them some kindness.

Even while it seems easy, it can be rather difficult to accomplish. Above and beyond for your ex and considering their needs are examples of kindness. You still need to do this even if you don't turn their world around.

Do not hold grudges.

Resentment is an indication that you are not forgiving. There are no winners in a breakup; you both lost the relationship. You must set aside the things that could irritate you about what your ex did.

It requires time.

The friendship thing takes time and patience to grow. It won't happen overnight. Additionally, give each other some room. Make sure your ex has ample room. It is difficult to realize that you no longer possess someone's heart, but miracles still occur over time and space.

Take out the green-eyed monster.

You shouldn't try to arouse your ex's jealousy right now. You may extinguish the small flame they had for you. Seeing someone else will make the ex feel horrible, as long as you were once in love. Thus, avoid attempting to convey to them how content you were without them, as I would question why you would want them back.

With them, spend time, but not all of your time.

You must make your former feel like they were missed, but this does not mean you spend all your time together. You will find yourself in embarrassing situations, and before you realize it, the same issues from your relationship will be rearing their head again. When a friendship develops into a relationship, you should ensure it has ground rules.

Not having sex with the ex.

You are forming a relationship here; thus, the two of you having sex is a major deal. Here, your head needs to rule your heart rather than vice versa. Maintaining your new status is essential, as reverting would merely result in hazy distinctions. Ensure it doesn't appear like you were using your friendship to get under their skin.

Not contacting

You'd better use tip number seven if you want to make sure tip number six works. No touching. Hugs are OK, but kissing, holding hands, and other similar actions are not.

Provide your assistance

If it's their birthday, send them your warmest wishes and perhaps even throw them a gift wrap. Encourage them if things aren't going well for them at work. You are aware of their values, and the truth is that a friend would be the one they would most like to be closest to.

Express your regret.

Recall that your ex is unaware of your decision to forgive. You must also own up to your mistakes. Express your regret to them for the times you behaved foolishly even though you knew better. Confession and admission have great significance in the reconciliation process.

Never fail to crack a joke on something from the past.

The best medicine has always been laughter. If you think back on the funniest and stupidest things you two ever did, you may always reminisce about the good old days. Making jokes like these shows your ex that you still cherish the memories you two had together.

Is Your Past Partner Willing To Give It Another Go?

Now that the boundaries of your relationship have finally been drawn, are you two, or have you already? You'd be shocked at how many relationships in the modern era still have hope for reconciliation. This report accuses the guys of attempting to patch things up with their ex-girlfriend.

Thus, continue reading if the time has arrived for you to see past the lines your ex-girlfriend paints for you. The most telling indicators that your ex-girlfriend wants you back will be highlighted in this post.

1. She maintains communication. Of all the signs, this one is arguably the most

evident. You begin to see patterns when your ex persistently bothers you, whether through regular text messages, phone calls, or simple e-mails. Had she truly determined that everything between you two is history, she wouldn't have communicated with you as frequently.

2. She continuously bumps into you. You will know something is wrong if you see your ex virtually everywhere you go, even at the mall or the same spots you used to hang out together. These are clear indications that she is missing you from your previous relationship. Therefore, if you notice that she is trying to visit you, you can be certain that this

indicates that, should the spark between you still exist, you should pursue a relationship with her.

3. She forces you to discuss your romantic life. You know she still has a crush on you if she brings up the issue of your love life practically every time you meet. Here, paying close attention to how she responds if you bring up other girls in your new life is important. If she acts like she's over you, you can be sure of it, but if she appears a bit agitated or even depressed when she shouldn't be, you can be sure she might still be interested in you.

4. She presents as though nothing occurred. If your former partner acts like she is still in your relationship,

remember that she may secretly be grieving the breakup. This is a fantastic chance to get back together if you feel the same way. Rather than rushing things, perhaps the best course of action in this case would be to take things one step at a time and let them unfold naturally.

5. She attempts to appear attractive to you. The last and most reliable clue to look for is if she makes an effort to act as you desire her to. You can now be certain that she sincerely wants you back. Maybe now that she knows how poorly she handled you, she wants to try to change so that you would find her more appealing. If you want her back, your best action is to simply follow her

lead and see where it takes you. Perhaps what you're both searching for is waiting for you at the end of the journey.

These are your five simple indicators that your ex-girlfriend is open to dating you again. Ultimately, it is up to you to determine whether or not you want her back.

Chapter 3: Is your ex someone you want back?

The three crucial inquiries you posed to yourself at the start of this book were: Have you moved on from your ex? You presumably believe you can skip this chapter if your response to the last question was "yes." However, this isn't the case at all.

Although relationships are among the most ambiguous aspects of life, there are legitimate reasons to win your ex back.

❖ Time for logic

Certain relationships endure and are thought to improve after two or three encounters. However, some partnerships are better left in the past and forgotten, while some are doomed from the beginning.

This chapter will help you determine whether your motives for wanting to reconcile with your ex-boyfriend are helping or hindering your prospects.

❖ You Still Have Feelings for Your Ex

This is most likely the main motivation for your desire to win your ex back. The outcomes are merely incidental. Right now, what counts is that you gave it your all. If things don't work out in the end, you won't have to suffer the anguish of constantly wondering what you could have done to get your ex-partner back.

❖ You Have Remorse About Your History

Although guilt can be as potent an incentive as love, it is not a sound excuse to win your ex back. You must learn to live with the guilt until time and forgiveness run out if there is no love. Guilt-driven reconciliation with your former partner can only cause further suffering.

❖ I'd like to give it another go.

It's not a terrible excuse, but it might not be the greatest one to get back together with your ex. You can fall in love again even though there may not be love for each or both of them. Should this cause your wish to reconcile with your former partner, exercise caution in asserting your desire. Lying can just make things worse between you and your former partner. Lying is never a solid foundation for a relationship.

❖ Now you are feeling guilty.

You weren't at fault when we split up.

But now that you know your former partner isn't doing well, you feel bad.

Although that makes sense, it's not a compelling enough argument to reconcile with your ex. You must delve deeper to see whether what you truly want to offer is company, an apology, or another chance at love. ▍You're by yourself.

Although it's not the worst justification for getting back together with your ex, it's undoubtedly one of the worst.

Seeking a relationship with your ex out of loneliness would be self-serving on your part.

Your reunion might be a godsend, but what about your former partner?

If your ex knew why you truly wanted to get back together, would he feel better?

Numerous alternative explanations might exist, and not all of them are reliable.

Not.

Ultimately, you must pay attention to your heart and your heart.

Is it truly what you want and the correct thing to do to get back together with your ex-boyfriend?

Chapter 2: WHAT REASONS AN EX TO RETURN

Of course, you should get back together with them. Still, how could your ex return to you if that wasn't their intention? There are several reasons, some of them are as follows:

- They are missing you.

It doesn't follow that they won't miss you because you and they split up. They probably remember many wonderful times spent with you with affection. They might also really miss your friendship.

- They genuinely adore you

The fact that they truly adore you makes them conceivable. Some forms of worship are profound and have eternal life.

This suggests that they may find denying their genuine affection for you difficult. They may have tried to go on, but they were unable to.

• They feel alone.

This isn't the greatest excuse for your ex to get back together. By any length of the imagination, it's anything but a decent one. Feeling hopeless should not be a reason to return to a failing relationship. But for some, it serves as an explanation for why they carry it out.

• Either they or you have changed.

If you were the one who made the most mistakes during the relationship, maybe they may give you another chance since they believe you have grown. Conversely, even if they were the ones who made the mistake, they have grown and evolved.

• They are unable to imagine life without you.

In the unlikely event that they truly love and miss you, they most likely won't be able to imagine their life without you.

In any case, they can be attached to you and unable to let go of their dream of the two of you being together forever.

WHAT IS THE TIME FRAME FOR AN EX-BOY TO RETURN?

Nobody can ever fully understand how difficult it is to go past someone.

You know you deserve your former partner back, but you have no idea how long it will take. Every person is different, and their situation is, too.

When you bid your partner a final goodbye, you may need time apart to process the situation and decide. The most difficult thing is getting past the depressing separation stage and deciding what to do immediately.

You should keep going, but before you take that step, there's a ton of work you want to accomplish to get back with your ex.

We first ask you to reflect carefully on your separation and identify your feelings. In the unlikely event that you truly need to start over with your ex after everything, we are here to support you.

We understand that you are eager to get back together and are still considering how long it will take to get your ex back. In any case, we advise persistence. Things cannot be hurried when other people are also engaged.

Many people will assure you that you won't be able to get your ex back for two to six months. Be that as it may, we shall choose an alternate tactic.

We'll talk about different kinds of separations and how long it may theoretically take to get your ex back.

Since every situation and person is different, as we have previously stated, it is practically impossible to tell you the exact time. Still, we can help you understand how long it might take to get your ex back.

Here are the various situations and the estimated time frames for receiving your separation.

- Joint segregation

The possibility of reuniting with your ex and shared separations is pleasant. You can get back together quickly in case you both decide that the decision to separate was inappropriate. The primary time investment needed to identify your problems will be needed.

Before continuing, you should resolve every issue; otherwise, there will be no point in making things right. Give your ex a month's notice before thinking about getting back together.

Take some time to evaluate your deep state. Can we presume that you are ready to get back together? Consider that for yourself. Do you think your ex will be interested in regularly resolving your conflicts?

Before moving further, you truly want to know the answers to these questions. Talk to your ex if you have distanced yourself from each other following the breakup. Make an effort to ascertain their mindset. When you reveal your feelings, consider how long your ex will take to respond.

Try not to rely too much on hoping your former partner will respond immediately. Almost half a month will be needed for that as well. Furthermore, there's always a chance that your ex should move on and not start over with you. When that happens, you should figure out how long it will take to pursue your former partner if you'd prefer not to give up after the initial "no."

So, if the split was amicable and normal and you both need to get back together, it can take at least two months. In addition, let's say you need your ex back, but he doesn't know. This could take up to four months.

- When your former partner unloaded you

You initiated the breakup, but now you want your former partner back? Since you are the one who injured your ex, and you now have to make every effort to get them back, this can be a frustrating time.

Until then, you'll need some time to process what led to the breakup and why you believe getting back together is a wise move. Think about why you separated from your ex and fell in love with them.

I'm curious why you let go of your ex. Did your former partner treat you poorly, or would you say that you were too difficult to even consider managing?

You should be honest with yourself to start over.

Sadly, we sometimes think that we are grieving the loss of our former partner while we are feeling hopeless, but that may not always be the case.

When you break up with your ex, you suddenly find yourself empty-handed. You have alone time and don't have the foggiest idea of what to do. You might not need love, but just someone's organization.

Try not to confuse sadness with love.

Give yourself time to spend with your friends and family. This will give you an idea of whether you are depressed or still obsessed with your former partner. You miss your ex when you talk to them, even after a fantastic night out with your friends.

Another possibility is that you miss your former partner because you miss their thoughtfulness and affection. If that's the only thing, think again. Is it possible to say that you are grieving for your former partner, or are you just being considerate?

Would you have a similar sense of joy if you distinguish yourself from others? Understanding your relationship before estimating how long it will take to win your ex back is important.

After considering every possible scenario may take up to 90 days, provided you and your ex-partner truly want to get back together. What's more, eight months on the off chance that you both don't know and finding an opportunity to grasp your sentiments. Much will also depend on how successfully your ex responds to starting over and making things right.

What Caused The Split?

The utilization of cause and effect is one of the most popular problem-solving techniques. Breakups are absolutely not an exception. Whatever the problem is, figuring out what kind of problem it is is always the best place to start. As for your split, you should begin by determining what went wrong. You might want to try writing it down for future reference.

Considerations For Ascertaining The Cause Of A Breakup

True, the subheading sounds more like the section title of a thesis paper, but that's a positive thing. Although it can be challenging, analyzing a broken relationship is essential if you want to truly get your former back. You must find a way to let the past go, look at the big view, and grow from your mistakes.

Sincerity

When trying to figure out why a relationship ended, this is an excellent issue to take into account. Being objective and truthful about what truly happened and you are too emotionally invested in the regrettable event of the breakup to think logically. Keep in mind that you don't have to place blame for your partner's breakup simply because you understand why. That is not true at all. It's not important to figure out who was mistaken. Rather, concentrating on how you could do better the next time necessitates being forthright and truthful about the real reason behind your split.

It makes sense that since a romantic relationship comprises two people, the topic of your partner's contribution to the stability of your union will also come up. Remember to present things positively and be honest about the part your partner will be playing in improving your relationship.

As an illustration

It's true that you will spend extra time with your partner to show them how much you care.

False: You will work less hours so that you may spend more time with your partner.

Even if your goal and strategy may be synonymous, how you go about achieving them might make things better for both you and your ex. Of course, your ex is also exposed to the same.

It's true that your spouse will grow to comprehend your feelings. Your partner will not treat you disrespectfully, despite what you may believe.

In other words, it is possible to be both polite and sincere at the same time.

Give each other the benefit of the doubt when discussing or considering the reason for your breakup, and avoid using hurtful language.

Finalization

Splits don't always result from mutually agreed-upon decisions. At times, it can be completely skewed. If you were the one who was left in the dark and perplexed after the separation, you must first find closure. Hopefully, your former partner will willingly support you in your journey forward. If not, you can choose to either move on from the split or try to determine what went wrong on your own. Either way, you should try to keep your thoughts about your ex-partner neutral. That's obviously not the place to start if you're looking for reconciliation.

Avoid Being Reliant

Following the breakup, you can think that something went wrong. When awful things happen to us, we often blame ourselves for them.

At times, we can place the blame on ourselves, but when we are too desperate, it doesn't help much.

Of course, we would do anything to attract attention. The least you could do after a breakup is to resurface in your former partner's mind.

If you start to feel needy, your attempts will not heal the deep gulf between you and your ex; rather, they will make it worse.

However, we were unable to simply resist this temptation. You'd have to figure out how to make up for the hole in your heart as the breakup starts to take an emotional toll.

It seems that there are ways to accomplish this without experiencing extreme despair.

Give it some time.

Let's be honest. You are willing to go to any lengths to save your relationship with your ex because you still adore them.

Once more, this makes things worse. All your ex can see is how desperate you are and how you simply cannot function without her in your life.

Rather, make an effort to accept the breakup with reason. This involves striving to improve yourself and comprehend the reasons that prompted the breakup.

You may need to wait till things settle down if you are really invested in getting the relationship back together. During this time, fight off any urge to think about your ex and focus on readying yourself for the big comeback instead.

Don't Tell, Show

Under no circumstances should you try to contact your ex via text, email, or phone! Trying to persuade her that you're capable of improving as a boyfriend. This merely demonstrates your desperation, and it will make it much simpler for your ex to go on.

Make every effort to never promise anything. It's likely that you will fall short of what your ex expected of you.

Throughout the separation, dedicate some time to improving yourself. Give up or cut back on some habits and go about your daily life as usual.

Your buddies might have informed your ex that you are open to bettering yourself, so you won't have to bother her with vague pledges.

Never bring up the breakup.

One sensual tip to keep in mind is to never bring up your breakup.

Never attempt to bring up the breakup, whether you are with friends or relatives. Once more, this will just highlight how vulnerable you are to the pressure of your own feelings. This kind of thinking suggests that you're not quite ready to go back on track.

Tell folks you're doing good and you hope your ex is doing well, too, if they inquire about your well-being following the breakup. Not a bit more than that.

Remain relaxed and informal. You are not in a position to complain or ask for help. Give yourself some time to recuperate and let your feelings subside.

Be enigmatic

The question "How is my ex doing?" has been bothering you both since the first day of the aftermath.

You're both making a lot of effort not to talk to each other during the breakup. This is the phase of transition when the temperature is allowed to drop to bearable levels. Attitude problems are being addressed at this time, and mutual animosity is lessening.

In light of the fact that you would prefer to remain anonymous for the time being and keep your ex guessing, your lines of communication with them are now momentarily closed in order to prevent interfering with their "emotional healing." Never forget that allure is equal to mystery.

Select "Underground"

Limiting access to your social media accounts, which entails limiting your tweets and Facebook wall posts, is one way to achieve this. If you truly feel compelled to divulge every aspect of your everyday existence, proceed with caution. Never publish anything about the breakup on social media, overtly or covertly. In this manner, you might pique your ex's interest without giving yourself away.

Recognizing the Indications

If you continue to hide for a long, your ex's curiosity will only pique. Her need to know compels her to look for information from other sources.

You might use your family or friends as a relay system. Your former partner will make an effort to inquire about their well-being and attempt to move on. This is true!

Additionally, try not to impart too much information to your friends or family. Again, provide evasive responses that are difficult to understand. Simply respond with "Fine" or "I'm doing well" if someone from your close-knit circle of acquaintances asks, "How are you taking all this in?"

Although it's difficult to analyze such responses, your ex is even more intrigued by them.

Feelings in Motion

If you're still thinking about getting back together with your ex, keep in mind that a breakup is just a temporary situation.

Your ex may try to stifle your longing for intimacy, but you still have that affection.

However, we couldn't rule out the chance that she might be going through the same emotional vacuum you are.

Your former partner might want to provide answers to certain queries.

Women need time to wonder about you; give it to her. By remaining withdrawn and limiting your online and physical presence, your ex will discover how different life is without you in it. Staying anonymous for so long will give her enough time to think twice about being your partner. Understand that as time passes, people start to think less of the hurt, anger, and negative emotions and more of what is good.

There will be times when your former partner is really missing you. Reuniting may not be far off in the future.

Your report on damages

The next step is to create a damage report. Be honest and forthright about what you did or said that could have a bad effect on your relationship going forward. Did you cheat on her? If so, she was right to dump you; there will be no point in pleading with her; you will have to prove yourself to her and change if you truly want her back.

A woman wants you to be more of a man than she is, and in my experience, a guy overpressurizes the girl 99% of the time, which leads to her acting weak, insecure, and needy. Masculine energy is not about being submissive or uncertain; rather, it is about purpose, drive, being goal-oriented, direct, and certain.

You most certainly followed suit.

Your ex will test you, and the more you mess up, the harder and longer the tests will be, but you will be ready for this. Should you cry, beg, blow up her phone, or call her friends, things will get pretty bad and she will make you pay. The more of your weak and insecure side you showed, the more she will make you pay for it.

Getting her to reassess you will be the easy part; getting a different value than the last time will be the hard part. This can be likened to grocery shopping; you make your decision fairly quickly if you have to choose between products; the rest of the time, however, you will be searching for proof that you have made the right decision; it is rare to admit that you have made a mistake in judgment.

You need to be better than you were when you first got to know her—not a people-pleaser, but a better version of yourself—and you need to be the best version of yourself that she has ever seen!

This phase is about owning up to your past mistakes, including your weak behavior during the breakup and in the past. It's about actively addressing your weak behavior going forward and letting go of your fear of being abandoned.

One person begins to change and the other finds it difficult to accept it: People's needs in relationships change as they mature and develop, and when one begins to change and the other finds it difficult to accept it, tension and conflict can arise.

The best way to handle this situation is to talk to your spouse openly about how you're feeling and why you're not comfortable with the current state of affairs. If they can't accept you for who you are, it's probably not worth it to stay in the relationship.

Abuse or violence: This is a clear deal-breaker; there's no justification for abuse or violence, and it will only cause you additional suffering. The best course of action is to end the relationship as soon as possible.

The best course of action for anyone in an abusive relationship is to leave; do whatever it takes to get away from your abuser. There are a lot of resources available to assist victims of domestic violence, so please don't be afraid to ask for assistance.

Substance abuse: When one person is hooked to drugs or alcohol, it's hard for them to maintain good relationships. Substance addiction is another deal-breaker and usually indicates that the relationship is doomed.

Solution: The best thing you can do for your safety and well-being or alcohol is to end it. There are a lot of support groups and resources available for people who are dealing with substance abuse issues. Don't try to handle this on your own – get help from professionals who understand addiction and recovery.

You and your ex can still salvage your relationship if you are both prepared to put in a lot of effort and make some concessions. Don't give up on your relationship just because something went wrong; there's always hope!

Should I apologize?

You made a mistake, you said you were sorry, but are you unsure if you should apologize again?

When someone asks for forgiveness and apologizes, it feels redundant to offer another apology because eventually people just say sorry out of habit rather than meaning it. It may even come across as insincere. This is a common question from people who want their ex back quickly and with the least amount of drama. The answer is that you only need to apologize once.

Though they might still be hurt by your actions, at least now there are no negative feelings remaining between the two of us. What if they apologize back? If they do, that's great! If not, then just respond with something like "thank you and sorry for hurting you too. I love you so much and hope we can move forward in the right way together. Can I call or text you later to talk more about it?"

It's usually better to seek professional treatment if someone is constantly apologizing and not giving them a chance to make up for their faults. This suggests that there may be another issue going on (such as depression or anger issues).

You can make new friends at free pen pal spots Easily. Making new friends online is good because you and your friends can learn from each other. The process of making online Friends is easy and simple. You simply subscribe to a profile to introduce yourself. You can indeed add some prints. The coming step is to stay until your profile is approved. You can also search for original and transnational friends you want. Also, you shoot a communication to people you've planted online. However, you can write them back and go from there, If they respond to your communication. There's no limit to how numerous people you can communicate with one day. Free penpals online service is what you need to look for new friends on the Internet.

These days, it's common to meet new friends on free penpals sites. You can connect with a large number of people by sending them a message. A pen pals service isn't about dating, because it's only focused on friendship. You can make new friends easily and readily. There's no cost to create a profile, look for friends, and communicate with them. You can meet original people in person, but you have to be comfortable initially. Some people enjoy making transnational friends in order to learn about other countries, similar in terms of language, culture, etc. Free online penpals services are the tool to meet new friends.

Making new friends on the Internet is largely dependent on your profile. We advise you to include information about your hobbies, aspirations, career, romantic status, family, age, and so on. If someone is interested in you, they will get in touch with you. Similarly, you can read other people's biographies and get in touch with them if you want to be friends. The free penpal service is what you need to connect with because you do not have to pay the class figure. You can make new friends in the comfort of your own home; you don't need to go anywhere in order to find friendships; all you have to do is turn on your computer and start looking for friends on the Internet.

Finding friends online at free penpals spots has become a miracle in the recent past. Some people find it awkward to meet new people in public. For these people, free penpals spots is a stylish way to meet new people online. You don't have to meet your new friends in person; all you have to do is write what you will say in communication and send it to your friends. Some long-term friends may even decide to get married. All you need is a profile to meet people online. A profile is a description of who you are. Essentially, it's a preface you write online to let people know about yourself. You can write anything you want. Finding friends online is quick and easy.

How to Easily Make Friends and Start Exchanges

Do you want to improve your conversational abilities and make friends quickly and easily? You can have this talent.

Both of these are quite easy to pick up and will help you feel more confident. Being able to speak comfortably to others can help you make friends and improve your fashion sense. Approaching someone and using a discussion starter is the first step in starting a conversation.

As an example, I recently went to a gathering where I approached a foreign person and said, "Hello. "That one little work was my discussion starter. Also, I followed up with a question, "What are you enjoying about this event?which sparked the conversation.

There are two things you should do when attempting to make friends: the first is to spend time getting to know the person you are trying to become friends with; the second is to identify the things you have in common. For example, I have friends with whom we discuss politics, others with whom we discuss sports, and still others with whom I can talk about anything because we are such close friends.

Spending time with others and discovering your common ground will help you become more comfortable introducing yourself and quickly form friendships once you have established common ground.

It's easy to initiate exchanges and form friendships. Just approach the other person, choose up a topic of conversation, and get to work talking. By focusing on your shared interests, you'll build stronger bonds with each other.

When Amicable Relationships Divorce

Even the strongest relationships can, regrettably, break down from time to time. However, there's always a reason for it, even if we can't always understand it at first.

There are a number of reasons why happy marriages fall apart and end in divorce. It's possible that your ex withdrew entirely and kept you in the dark about what was going on, or you might have learned this after putting up with pointless arguments.

Individuals in pain who are unclear about their partner's role in the relationship often find themselves reacting in a way that is completely at odds with what they should be doing to get their ex back.

In order for men to act in ways that make sense to them and for women to generally utilize techniques that appeal to them, certain circumstances must be satisfied.

Understanding that men and women think differently is a crucial lesson. Like utilizing feminine logic to win back a guy, using male logic to the challenge of winning back a female is frequently futile.

Men and women in these situations, despite their best efforts, often behave in ways that would unwittingly repel and push away the person they genuinely want to accept back into their lives. This is a truly unpleasant element of the scenario.

This suggests that they behave in a way that is completely at odds with what they ought to do in order to get their ex back and include them in their life once more.

Consider this. Is your present strategy working to win your ex back? Or does it just make you feel worse by putting distance between you and that person?

Let's examine some of the things that both sexes consider when in a relationship and how they interpret their partners' behavior.

These realizations often result in a far better comprehension of both what went wrong in the relationship and what to do when good relationships go apart.

Beautiful, solid partnerships can bring two individuals a tremendous lot of happiness and fulfillment. But when good relationships end, the hurt can be unbearable and long-lasting.

The breakdown of a relationship sometimes results from a multitude of neglected or unresolved issues. Maintaining a relationship takes time, careful communication, and work; if they are overlooked, the relationship could terminate suddenly.

Finding the root causes of broken relationships is crucial, as is approaching each issue head-on with an open mind and heart. In certain cases, something as simple as a misunderstanding or a communication error could have caused the collapse. It could be more difficult in other circumstances and include more severe issues like trust or treachery.

Whatever the case, it's imperative to learn from the failure and ensure that similar issues don't lead to another one in the future.

This can mean just getting to know each other's intentions better or maintaining open lines of communication at all times in order to rebuild trust. Although it takes time and effort to build strong relationships, sometimes even the best-laid plans backfire.

It's critical to take lessons from these failures in order to prevent repeating the same mistakes. With some time, effort, and understanding, two people may mend a strong connection and make it even stronger than it was before.

Understanding that trust must be restored is essential to repairing a damaged relationship.

This can be achieved by taking care of the issues that led to the split and making sure that each partner feels secure and protected in the relationship.

This may mean being open and honest with one another, as well as being aware of one another's needs.

Being patient and understanding of each other's feelings is also essential for the relationship to heal and trust to be rebuilt.

Regretfully, there are instances when a relationship ends irrevocably. It's important to remember that moving on and finding pleasure elsewhere is quite okay when this happens. There is no right or wrong decision when it comes to partnerships—what matters is that each partner is devoted to their own wants and self.

Nevertheless, even in healthy relationships, upkeep requires work and dedication. Maintaining a strong connection and preventing its disintegration requires effort and comprehension. Both sides need to put forth equal effort to keep the relationship going and deal with any problems that may arise.

Try to keep the conversation light-hearted at first, but it's acceptable to "let it slip" that you occasionally have thoughts about the individual in issue. This is very important.

It's also important to end the conversation by stating that you'd like to catch up later.

Chapter 6: Have Honesty

It's likely that your former partner will be able to tell if you are acting genuinely or if you are just acting for fun. You will lose every opportunity to reconcile with him or her if they believe you are doing the latter.

Express Your Thoughts and Mean What You Say

After six months of dating, Jane made the decision to end things with Shane. She tells Shane that she thought he wasn't paying enough attention to their relationship. Shane made the decision to woo Jane once more a month after their breakup, telling her that he would change and treat her with the respect she deserves.

To let Jane know he has been thinking of her and that he misses her, Shane began by sending her brief SMS and emails. Two weeks later, he called to see how she was doing rather than making a date request. Given that tulips are Jane's favoriteflower, he knew to send a bouquet of them to her office the following day.

Shane thought it would be a good idea to try asking Jane out for a casual meal to catch up after a few more weeks of courtship. Jane accepted Shane's invitation after witnessing the work he had put in to win her back.

Sincerity is Essential.

Be truthful in all you do. To achieve this, make use of the advice listed below:

Be straightforward but kind in your SMS messages rather than overflowing with flowery, pointless jargon.

Simply to let your ex know that they are on your mind, give them a call. In order to avoid bothering your ex or taking up too much of their time, keep the call brief.

Send your ex little mementos or gifts to let them know you still care. Give her a bunch of flowers and some chocolates as a surprise. Give him a cup of his preferred tea or coffee. Keep your offerings uncomplicated and uncomplicated. Sending something too elaborate could cause your ex to misinterpret you and believe you are attempting to win back their love. Recall, there are advantages to simplicity.

It's crucial to demonstrate to your former partner that you genuinely want to make amends. This entails being sincere with yourself, understanding how you really feel, and communicating this to your former partner.

Chapter 7: The Influence of Memories

Reminding your ex of the good moments you two shared in the past is one of the best strategies to get them back. You have a better possibility of rekindling your passion with your former love if you do things right.

Vintage Music

Two months after their breakup, Jeffrey asked Tess to a casual supper in his apartment. Since then, he has been attempting to win Tess back, and while she has responded to his advances, she doesn't seem ready to reconcile.

Jeffrey prepared Tess's favorite dishes, including apple cinnamon pie, chicken

Alexander, and pesto linguini, to further his argument. In addition, he put created a playlist that included both of their joint favorite songs from their earlier years of dating Tess.

Jeffrey started playing the tune that had played during their first dance at the school ball when Tess arrived. With a smile and tears in her eyes, Tess told Jeffrey that she was amazed he could still recall.

After that, their food went down a treat.

A Flashback to the Past

The following are some strategies to capitalize on nostalgia:

Tell her in a brief text message how something reminded you of him/her. For instance, hello Ross. A Hello Kitty snow globe caught my eye recently in a store close to my workplace. It brought back memories of the occasion when we purchased one for your cousin. I just wanted to say that it brought a grin to my face ☺

Send along articles or reviews of the movies you saw together in the past. Another option is to try searching for snippets of your preferred scenes.

Provide them links to your best tracks, along with a brief explanation of why they stand out, if you have any.

Send vintage pictures of your travels or of the two of you having a good time hanging together. Avoid sharing too personal or amorous of pictures with him/her in case it turns them off.

You can give your ex a copy of a book you know they adore if they are a reader. Include a message describing how it brought him/her to mind.

Reminding your ex of your positive memories while minimizing the unpleasant ones is the key to keeping your relationship positive. Your ex will be more likely to give you two another chance if you reflect on the pleasant times you shared.

WHEN OTHERS' RELATIONSHIPS GO Wrong

What occurs if you abide by every guideline yet your former partner still keeps putting distance between you?

Sometimes relationships end with no apparent explanation at all. Your ex might have chosen to cease communicating with you, to stop responding to your texts, and to completely distance themselves from the relationship as if you never existed, even though you might have thought things were going great.

The individual who has completely withdrew from a relationship may have very different ideas about where the partnership was originally headed, but the person who has been shunned frequently feels they have done nothing wrong.

The truth is that people who experience love secrete a hormone that is extremely similar to that of those with OCD (obsessive compulsive disorder). This is one of the reasons why people who are in love find it difficult to eat, sleep soundly, concentrate at work, or think about anything but the person they are with.

Of course, this does not mean that your partner felt the same way at the same time as you. Just like not everyone feels hungry at the same time, not everyone experiences the same feelings at the same moment.

The awful thing about this is that occasionally one of the people in the relationship could think about taking it further. They'll ponder about various scenarios for a while, wondering what might occur once they get past the dating stage of their relationship.

This could lead one person to believe that the relationship has progressed beyond what it actually has, when in fact the other person might just be making an effort to comprehend their own feelings. There are times when this is called a "instant connection." One person is believing they are just dating, while the other is in full relationship mode and wondering why their partner doesn't appear to be reciprocating.

Trying to convince their partner that they should be together or that they are truly in love with them is the worst mistake someone can do in this situation. When they witness women responding in this way, males may feel compelled to slow down or even stop altogether, since they are left wondering what is going on. Because they believe their partner to be helpless and reliant, they may occasionally turn away from one another or even withdraw completely. A woman's desperation and insecurity turn men off.

But many men are guilty of treating the women they like the same way as well. They could try to convince her that he is a better fit for her because he loves her more than any other guy. These circumstances are problematic since it's hard for them to see that what they're doing wrong is wrong.

GO BACK TO THE STARTING TO FIND THE SOLUTION

Returning to the start of the relationship is almost always the best way to get your ex back.

How did your partner behave when you first met them? More importantly, how did you act in the early stages of your relationship?

Most likely, you were both acting appropriately. You both worked really hard to make sure the other person was happy with it. Furthermore, you would have both been driven to make a good impression on the other person and would not have seen any minor behavioral or personality defects. Now think back to your last conversation with your former partner. Did the two of you have a good interaction? Or did you quarrel, experience tension, anger, or worry about the other person's thoughts?

This mental image of you in his or her mind is probably one of you fighting, depressed, crying, and worried about the future of the relationship if you and your ex were not getting along. It is impossible to imagine optimistic thoughts of a bright future ahead of you both under this circumstance. Rather, they're probably thinking about how to meet someone who resembles the person they first saw you as.

Yes, you as you were the first time you met. He or she would have fallen in love with the joyful, confident, positive, energetic, independent person you were when you first met. You would have made him or her feel happy while they were with you, and they would have enjoyed wondering when you would find time in your busy schedule to come see them again.

What then changed?

www.ingramcontent.com/pod-product-compliance
Lightning Source LLC
Chambersburg PA
CBHW052141110526
44591CB00012B/1818